Quantum Mind Shifting

Harness the Power of Your Words to Leap in Consciousness and

Manifest Like a Pro

By

Theo Tilton

Copyright

For permission requests, write to the publisher, at

Theo Tilton Coaching,
45 S Park Place, Suite 143
Morristown, NJ 07960.

Visit the author's website at www.theotilton.com

Paperback ISBN: 978-1-7375746-5-1

Editing and formatting by Theo Tilton
Cover used with permission by Rob W. **@cal5086**

Disclaimer

This book provides general information about quantum physics, and discussions about consciousness, prayer, self-help, personal transformation, spirituality, performance, and related subjects. The advice and strategies contained herein may not be suitable for every situation. This work is sold with the understanding that the author and publisher are not engaged in rendering health, medical, legal, accounting, relationship or other professional services. Neither the author nor the publisher shall be liable for damages arising here from the fact that an organization or website is referred to in this work as a reference, citation or potential resource of further information does not mean the author or publisher endorses the information, contents, or organization the website may provide, or recommendations it may make. Further, readers should note the information and websites listed may have changed or have been deleted between the time when this book was written and when it was read. The information and other content provided in this book, or in any linked materials, are not intended and should not be construed as medical or psychological advice nor is the information a substitute for professional medical expertise or treatment. If you or any other person has a medical concern, you should consult with your health care provider or seek other professional medical treatment. Never disregard professional medical advice or delay in seeking it because of something that you have read in this book or in any linked materials. If you think you may have a medical emergency, call your doctor or emergency services immediately. The opinions and views expressed in this book, website, and other materials obtained through OpenAl, ChatGPT have no relation to those of any legal, accounting, professional service, academic, hospital, physical, or mental health practice or other institution.

This book was written by Theo Tilton, Quantum Mindshift Coach. Published by Theo Tilton Coaching in collaboration with the most powerful tools available in Artificial Intelligence. Email: theo@theotilton.com

Join the QMS Collective Community and contact the author for further support.

Welcome to the Quantum Mind Shifting Collective – a vibrant community of like-minded individuals dedicated to unlocking the secrets of the universe and manifesting their wildest dreams. As the author of "Quantum Mind Shifting: Harness the Power of Your Words to Leap in Consciousness and Manifest Like a Pro," I am thrilled to invite you to join this transformative group.

Click or type link to Join the QMS Collective Community

🔗 https://www.facebook.com/groups/qmscollective/

Here, you'll find a supportive space where you can connect with fellow seekers, share insights, and embark on a journey of personal growth and discovery. Whether you're new to the world of quantum mindset or a seasoned practitioner, the QMS Collective offers a wealth of resources, including exclusive content, live events, and group coaching sessions. Don't miss out on this opportunity to be part of a community that is revolutionizing the way we think, feel, and create. Join the QMS Collective today and take the first step towards manifesting your dreams!

Warm regards,
Theo Tilton

Experience a QMS LIVE Session for yourself.

If you want to experience a professional QMS Leap Session. Schedule a personal one-on-one session with Theo Tilton, a seasoned Life Coach and Quantum Mindset Expert, and unlock the full potential of your consciousness. Whether you're looking to overcome limiting beliefs, manifest your deepest desires, or navigate life's challenges with grace and confidence, Theo's personalized guidance and support will empower you to create lasting transformation in every area of your life. Don't wait any longer to unleash your inner power and live the life you've always dreamed of. Reach out today and take the first step towards a brighter, more abundant future.

Set up a LIVE Personal QMS Session by typing the following link into your browser or clicking here:

https://tinyurl.com/Services-by-Theo

Dedication

This book is dedicated to my beloved. Thank you for believing in me, accepting me and all my flaws, supporting me in all my dreams, and trusting I'll just get shit done. You mean the world to me, and I have all these same qualities for you. Just when I was starting to lose hope in Love, as if a by a miracle in one last ditch effort to express self-love towards myself, you showed up like an angel that answered my prayer. You are my muse, you are my love, you are my inspiration, you are my heart and so much more. I look forward to a lifetime of love, growth, and expansion.

Intention

My intention with 'QMS Quantum Mind Shifting' is to introduce this transformative practice on a global scale, ensuring that its power is accessible to individuals of all backgrounds and beliefs. This book serves as a spiritual tool to complement and fortify existing beliefs, rather than promoting any specific faith. The principles of quantum science presented within these pages are intended to enhance readers' understanding of their own spiritual journey and empower them to create positive change in their lives.

I aim to impact the lives of 1 million individuals through the teachings of QMS, awakening humanity to its spiritual significance within the universe. By embracing our innate ability to create, grow, heal, and prosper, we can foster harmonious communities and a world that works for everyone. My vision is for all beings to experience abundance, optimal health, love, and freedom, contributing to a collective flourishing in the cosmos.

Through 'QMS Quantum Mind Shifting,' my goal is to inspire a profound shift in consciousness, guiding readers towards a life filled with joy, fulfillment, and abundance.

What Others Are Saying:

"I worked recently with Theo Tilton. And he coached me through a process of reaching a goal that I wasn't sure was possible. Theo's tried and true methods, his absolute unwavering belief, and his ability to manifest like anything from nothing. Not only did I reach my goal, when I look back, I'm like, that wasn't hard. I am absolutely convinced that it was Theo's belief, his quantum magical self, that turned it into a reality. I took the steps. I took the action. I worked my butt off, but Theo was the container. He was the energy and I am so grateful for him. If you have the opportunity to work with Theo on any project or to receive coaching from him, get it, run, do not walk, he will turn your life into a magical spectacle."

✪ ✪ ✪ ✪ ✪ - Trista Polo.

"My more recent experiences with QMS, scientific prayer have been exciting and fruitful. It hasn't been just about learning the law of attraction but truly a step-by-step process in how to use the power of your words to manifest the life of your dreams. I have experienced everything from healing in the body, being able to sell my home very quickly and finding another home quickly and easily. I trust that if you use this process the way I have you will be manifesting like a pro as well. Theo is the master of this process and has been perfecting the art and science of manifesting the life you want to live."

✪ ✪ ✪ ✪ ✪ - Trey Isenhower

"My wife and I have been communicating extremely well. We are extremely grateful for Theo's workshop and the Time Machine Exercise. Buying Theo's book, has been a great investment."

⭐⭐⭐⭐⭐ - Juan Diego & Marina Santamaria

"Working with Theo's QMS method has accelerated my manifestation in business and life. Theo is the coach you want to hire to take you to that next level of Quantum Leap success in your life! I highly recommend you contact him ASAP! You will be glad you did."

⭐⭐⭐⭐⭐ - Luis S

"Theo's, QMS is energizing, and exciting. He will teach you to make spiritual mind treatment a habit. Through using it, you will gain a whole new, vantage point, or "SHIFT."

Liken it to climbing a mountain and not seeing anything amazing. Then, taking a few more steps up, and realizing an entire panorama of beauty and amazement, almost a surrealist that is now your reality (that had you not gone three more steps, you may have missed).

Your goals and dreams are on an attainable path. This will enable you to access them, circumventing roadblocks."

⭐⭐⭐⭐⭐ - Bashi R.

"Before I even knew about QMS I had a lot of anxiety around flying on airplanes. I would be stuck in traffic leaving 3 to sometimes 4 hrs before the flights and yet I get stuck in the worst traffic in an uber waiting for hours to get to the airports. There have been moments that the planes were being boarded. What could have gone wrong did go wrong? After years of these types of freak occurrences my friends would tease me that I somehow cause these endless strings of delays.

Theo did a QMS session over the phone while I was stuck in the Uber racing to the airport and all of a sudden traffic cleared as if there were an email sent to all drivers in front of me to turn off to other streets. I arrived to the airport on time hassle free. The lady at the counter asked if I was Bailey and they have been looking for me. I went through security faster than ever and arriving at the gate just in time to board. The weirdest thing is that my back pain stop happening on flights. QMS works"

✪ ✪ ✪ ✪ ✪ - Bailey L

Preface

In the vast expanse of the cosmos, where time and space intertwine in an intricate dance of energy and matter, there exists a profound truth that has captivated the minds of scientists and philosophers throughout the ages. It is the truth of consciousness—a boundless sea of awareness that permeates every corner of the universe, from the smallest subatomic particle to the grandest galaxies swirling in the cosmic expanse.

At the heart of this cosmic symphony lies a revelation that transcends the confines of human understanding. It is the revelation that we are not separate from the universe, but rather integral parts of its majestic tapestry—a truth echoed by the ancient wisdom of spiritual traditions and the cutting-edge discoveries of modern science.

Consider for a moment the remarkable parallels between the macrocosm and the microcosm—the cosmic dance of galaxies and solar systems mirroring the swirling motion of atoms and molecules on a planetary scale. It is a breathtaking realization that reminds us of our profound connection to the cosmos—to the very fabric of existence itself.

In this cosmic theater of existence, each of us is a living expression of the divine—a unique amalgamation of stardust and starlight, molded in the image and likeness of the universe itself. From the vast expanse of space to the intricate dance of atoms within our bodies, we are manifestations of the same divine essence—a truth that lies at the core of our being, waiting to be rediscovered and embraced.

It is within this sacred space of interconnectedness that the power of Quantum Mind Shifting (QMS) resides—a transformative practice that empowers us to tap into the infinite potential of the quantum field and shape our reality in alignment with our deepest desires and highest aspirations.

As we embark on this journey of self-discovery and exploration, let us remember that we are not mere observers of the universe, but active participants in its unfolding drama. Let us embrace the truth of our divine nature and awaken to the boundless possibilities that lie within us, waiting to be unleashed and realized.

So let us dive deep into the mysteries of consciousness and together, let us unlock the secrets of the universe and harness the power of QMS to create a reality filled with love, joy, and abundance.

Does this sound familiar? Meet Sarah.

Sarah was once a vibrant and driven individual, full of passion and ambition. She had dreams of making a difference in the world, of building a successful career, and of finding love and fulfillment in her personal life. But somewhere along the way, life took an unexpected turn, and Sarah found herself struggling in almost every area of her life.

In her career, Sarah felt stuck in a dead-end job that offered little fulfillment or opportunity for growth. Despite her best efforts, she struggled to advance in her field, and the constant stress and pressure took a toll on her mental and emotional well-being.

In her relationships, Sarah faced a similar sense of stagnation and disappointment. She longed for deep connections and meaningful companionship, but her attempts always seemed to end in heartbreak or disillusionment. She felt alone, isolated, and unsure if she would ever find the love and connection she craved.

On top of it all, Sarah struggled with her own inner demons – self-doubt, insecurity, and a lingering sense of inadequacy that seemed to follow her wherever she went. No matter how hard she tried to push past these feelings, they always seemed to resurface, holding her back from realizing her full potential and living the life she truly desired.

But just when Sarah felt like she was at her lowest point, something miraculous happened. She stumbled upon a mystical practice known as Quantum Mind Shifting (QMS), a powerful method that promised to unlock the secrets of the universe and transform her life in unimaginable ways.

Intrigued by the promise of healing and transformation, Sarah began to explore the principles of QMS and how they could apply to her own life. With each step she took on her QMS journey, she felt a shift in the very fabric of reality around her. Opportunities began to present themselves seemingly out of thin air, and miraculous coincidences started to unfold at every turn.

As she delved deeper into the practice of QMS, Sarah discovered a newfound sense of empowerment and connection to the universe. She learned how to harness the power of her own consciousness to manifest her deepest desires and bring her wildest dreams to life.

Slowly but surely, Sarah began to see the fruits of her labor. She found the courage to pursue new opportunities in her career, leading to greater success and fulfillment than she had ever imagined possible. In her relationships, she experienced a profound sense of connection and intimacy, as if the universe itself was conspiring to bring her the love and companionship she had always longed for.

But perhaps most importantly, Sarah discovered a sense of inner peace and self-acceptance that she had never known before. Through QMS, she learned to trust in the magical and mystical forces at work in the universe, knowing that she was always supported and guided on her journey.

Does Sarah's story resonate with you? Have you ever felt the call of the mystical and the magical, longing to tap into the infinite possibilities of the universe? If so, perhaps it's time to explore the transformative potential of QMS and unlock a brighter, more enchanted future for yourself.

Who is This Book For?

If you picked-up this book, chances are you are a proactive individual who is seeking to transform your own life and learn how to powerfully manifest your dreams with the help of QMS. You are open-minded, curious, and committed to personal growth and self-improvement. Chances are you have already explored various self-help modalities, such as mindfulness, meditation, and positive affirmations, but are now ready to delve deeper into the transformative power of quantum principles.

Quantum seekers are likely to be someone who feels a sense of discontent or stagnation in certain areas of their life, whether it's their career, relationships, health, or overall well-being. They may be experiencing challenges such as stress, anxiety, self-doubt, or a lack of clarity about their goals and purpose. Despite any obstacles they may face, quantum seekers possess a strong desire for positive change and a belief in their ability to create the life they desire.

If you are still reading you are also likely to resonate with the teachings of spiritual and metaphysical concepts, such as the law of attraction, universal energy, and the interconnectedness of all things. You are seeking practical tools and guidance to harness these principles and apply them in their everyday life to manifest your intentions and desires.

You are ready to embrace new perspectives, adopt empowering beliefs, and take inspired action to align with your highest potential.

Let's unlock this valuable resource on your path to living a truly extraordinary life.

Unlocking the Power of QMS

Welcome to a transformative journey unlike any other, where you are about to embark on a profound exploration of QMS and its extraordinary potential to reshape your reality and manifest your deepest desires.

At its core, this book is a roadmap for your personal transformation, offering you a comprehensive blueprint for harnessing the power of your mind to create new realities and unlock your full potential. Through a combination of cutting-edge insights from quantum physics, ancient spiritual wisdom, and practical techniques, you will learn how to tap into the infinite possibilities of the quantum field and manifest the life you truly desire.

Your journey begins with an introduction to the foundational principles of QMS, providing you with a solid understanding of how new realities are generated and the role of your consciousness in shaping your experiences. From there, you will dive into the practical application of QMS techniques, guided step-by-step through the five stages of Quantum Identification, Quantum Entanglement, Quantum Realization/Declaration, Quantum Thanksgiving and Gratitude, and Release and Surrender to the Quantum Foam (Somethingness from Nothingness)

But this book goes beyond mere theory—it's a hands-on guide to real-world transformation. You will have the opportunity to put your newfound knowledge into practice through workbook exercises, sample QMS scripts, and troubleshooting tips for overcoming common challenges.

Whether you're seeking to manifest abundance, improve relationships, enhance health, or achieve any other goal, "The QMS Blueprint" offers you a comprehensive framework for unlocking the limitless potential of your mind and creating the life you truly desire. Get ready to embark on a journey of discovery, empowerment, and transformation with QMS as your guide.

Contents

Introduction

Defining The Basics of QMS

"The reason we aren't experiencing the life we want is due to a quantum alignment problem in consciousness" – Theo Tilton

Hey there, fellow seekers of transformation! Let's dive into the world of QMS and uncover its profound connection to quantum physics, drawing parallels with the teachings of Ernest Holmes' Science of Mind.

In Ernest Holmes' timeless classic, "The Science of Mind," he introduced the concept of spiritual mind treatment as a powerful tool for aligning our thoughts with our desired outcomes (Holmes, 1926). This practice invites us to recognize the incredible creative power of our minds and use affirmative prayer to manifest positive change in our lives.

Now, let's fast forward to the present and explore QMS, a transformative practice that takes inspiration from Holmes' teachings and infuses them with insights from quantum physics (Tiller, 2007). QMS is all about harnessing the power of consciousness to shape our reality. It's about recognizing that our thoughts and intentions have a direct impact on the quantum field, influencing the outcomes we experience.

But QMS is more than just a technique—it's a personal journey of ascension in consciousness. It's about raising our level of mind and using our words to increase the vibration and frequency of our limitations, thoughts, beliefs, boundaries, and self-image. Through the practice of QMS, we elevate our consciousness, aligning ourselves with higher frequencies and opening the door to greater possibilities.

My own journey into Quantum began in college, where I was first exposed to the fascinating concepts of quantum physics. It sparked a curiosity within me about the nature of reality, God, and the universe. A decade later, I discovered the work of Ernest Holmes and the Science of Mind, which further deepened my understanding of these concepts. I realized that Holmes, along with other luminaries of the Transcendentalist movement, had tapped into profound truths about the nature of existence, which I now integrate into what I call QMS.

In essence, QMS is a practice of empowerment. It's about stepping into our true power as co-creators of our reality and shaping our lives according to our deepest desires. By embracing the principles of quantum mechanics and the wisdom of spiritual teachings, we embark on a journey of self-discovery and transformation, unlocking the limitless potential of our minds and more specifically, our WORD.

Basics of Quantum Physics

Before we dive into the enchanting world of QMS, let's take a moment to lay down the groundwork by unraveling the fascinating mysteries of quantum physics. Quantum physics is like the superhero of science – diving deep into the tiniest building blocks of the universe and blowing our minds with its mind-bending discoveries. So, grab your mental magnifying glass, put on your thinking caps and let's embark on this adventure together!

Key Theories, Experiments, and Real-Life Impact:

1. Superposition:
   - *Theory:* Alright, so picture this: a particle can be in, like, a gazillion states at once until someone actually checks on it. It's like Schrödinger's cat – chilling in a box, both alive and dead, until we open the lid and

reveal its fate.

- *Experiment:* Now, imagine shining light through two tiny slits onto a screen. Sounds simple, right? Well, the Double-Slit Experiment showed that light can act like a wave and a particle at the same time, creating a funky pattern on the screen. Mind = blown!

- *Real-Life Impact:* Understanding superposition means realizing that things aren't always as they seem. Just like particles, our lives can be full of possibilities until we make a choice. It's a reminder to embrace uncertainty and keep our minds open to endless opportunities.

2. Entanglement:
   - *Theory:* Brace yourself for some serious mind-bending stuff. Entanglement is like when two particles become BFFs and start dancing to the same rhythm, no matter how far apart they are. It's like having a cosmic connection that defies the laws of space and time.

   - *Experiment:* Picture this – Einstein, Podolsky, and Rosen sitting around, pondering the fate of entangled particles. Their EPR Paradox proposed that measuring one particle instantly affects its entangled buddy, even if they're light-years apart. Crazy, right?

   - *Real-Life Impact:* Entanglement teaches us the power of connection, showing that we're never truly alone in this vast universe. It's a reminder to cherish our relationships and recognize the invisible threads that bind us to one another.

Uncertainty Principle:

- ***Theory:*** Get ready to embrace some quantum fuzziness! The Uncertainty Principle says we can't know everything about a particle at once. It's like trying to pin down a slippery eel – the more you know about its position, the fuzzier its momentum becomes.

- ***Experiment:*** Stern and Gerlach decided to play around with some silver atoms and a magnetic field. The result? Atoms going all wonky and showing us that we can't measure certain things with absolute precision. Talk about keeping us on our toes!

- ***Real-Life Impact:*** The Uncertainty Principle reminds us to embrace the unknown and find comfort in ambiguity. Life isn't always black and white, and that's okay. It's about learning to navigate the gray areas with grace and flexibility

  .

Wave-Particle Duality:

- ***Theory:*** Hold onto your hats, folks – things are about to get wavy! Wave-particle duality says that particles can be both solid and squiggly at the same time. It's like having a split personality, but in a quantum kind of way. |

- ***Experiment:*** Davisson and Germer fired some electrons at a nickel target and got a surprise – a groovy diffraction pattern, just like waves in a pond. Who knew electrons could be so chill?

- ***Real-Life Impact:*** Wave-particle duality challenges our perceptions of reality, reminding us that things aren't always what they seem. It's a wake-up call to embrace the complexities of life and appreciate the beauty of paradox.

Observer Effect:

- **Theory:** Alright, here's where things get trippy. The Observer Effect says that just by watching something, we can change its behavior. It's like having a superpower where our very presence alters the outcome of an experiment.

- **Experiment:** Picture this – some unsuspecting photons minding their own business until a scientist decides to peek at them. Suddenly, these photons start behaving differently, just because they know someone's watching. Talk about stage fright!

- **Real-Life Impact:** The Observer Effect highlights the power of perception and intention, showing that our thoughts and actions can shape our reality. It's a reminder to cultivate mindfulness and be conscious of the energy we bring into the world.

Well, there you have it – a crash course in the mind-bending world of quantum physics! Now that we've wrapped a portion of our heads around these mind-blowing concepts, let's jump into all of the benefits of using this powerful practice, QMS.

Benefits of Practicing QMS:

After working with hundreds of clients for nearly a decade, I have witnessed firsthand the transformative power of QMS. Clients from all walks of life have reported experiencing profound changes in various aspects of their lives, thanks to their commitment to practicing QMS. From overcoming limiting beliefs to manifesting their deepest desires, the benefits of QMS are truly remarkable. Here are just a few of the benefits that clients have reported experiencing:

1. **Manifestation of Desires**: Align your thoughts and intentions with your desired outcomes to co-create the life you envision.

2. **Increased Consciousness**: Elevate your awareness and perception of reality, tapping into the interconnectedness of all things and the infinite potential of the quantum field.

3. **Enhanced Emotional Well-being**: Cultivate inner harmony and serenity by releasing limiting beliefs and negative thought patterns.

4. **Improved Relationships**: Attract more fulfilling and harmonious relationships by adopting a positive outlook and mindset.

5. **Heightened Creativity**: Unlock new ideas, insights, and innovations by tapping into the creative potential of the quantum field.

6. **Enhanced Problem-Solving Skills**: Develop a flexible and open-minded approach to problem-solving, finding creative solutions to challenges.

7. **Greater Resilience**: Navigate life's ups and downs with confidence and inner strength, developing resilience in the face of adversity.

8. **Overall Well-being**: Experience a deeper sense of meaning and satisfaction in life by aligning with your true purpose and highest potential.

9. **Physical Well-being**: Clients have reported tangible improvements such as decreased stress and anxiety, lowered blood pressure, and improved health.

10. **Love and Relationships**: Find love and start loving, accepting relationships, fostering deeper connections and intimacy.

11. **Career Fulfillment**: Quit jobs that are unfulfilling and discover or create careers that align with your passions and talents, leading to increased success and satisfaction.

12. **Freedom and Expression**: Experience newfound levels of freedom and expression, allowing you to live authentically and pursue your dreams.

13. **Healing**: Witness healing of diseases, ailments, and injuries, as QMS helps to restore balance and harmony to the body and mind.
14. **Transformation in Every Aspect of Life**: Nearly every aspect of life can be altered using QMS, from health and relationships to career and personal growth.

In essence, QMS offers limitless possibilities for personal transformation and growth. The universe is the limit, and the only boundary is the one you create in your mind. By embracing the principles of QMS, you can unlock your true potential and create the life of your dreams.

What can QMS be used for?

We as human being share 4 common areas where all situations/conditions/circumstances arise...

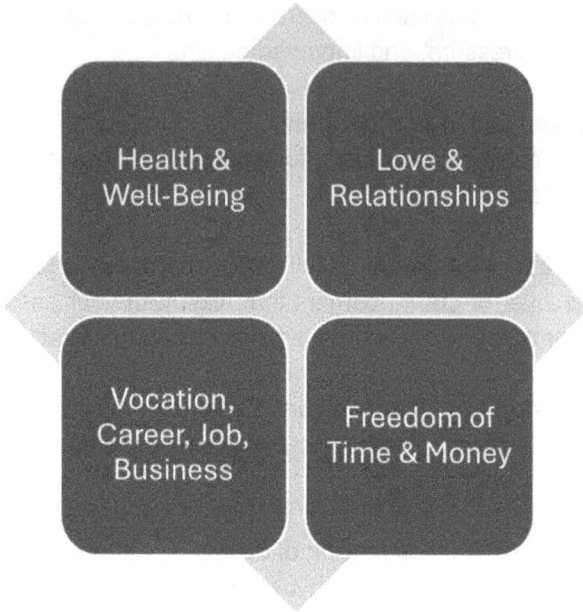

Health & Well-Being	Love & Relationships
Vocation, Career, Job, Business	Freedom of Time & Money

QMS can be used to intentionally impact these four common areas of life:

1. **Health & Well-Being:** QMS enables individuals to cultivate a positive mindset and emotional resilience, leading to improved overall health and well-being. By releasing stress, anxiety, and negative emotions through QMS practices, individuals experience greater vitality, energy, and physical wellness.

2. **Love & Relationships:** Through QMS, individuals enhance their capacity for love, compassion, and understanding, leading to deeper and more fulfilling relationships. By shifting limiting beliefs and patterns, individuals attract harmonious

connections and cultivate greater intimacy, trust, and mutual respect in their relationships.

3. **Vocation, Career, Business, or Job:** QMS empowers individuals to align with their true purpose and passion, leading to greater success and fulfillment in their vocation, career, business, or job. By clarifying their goals, intentions, and vision, individuals leverage the power of QMS to manifest opportunities, overcome challenges, and achieve their professional aspirations.

4. **Time & Money Freedom:** Through QMS, individuals transform their relationship with time and money, experiencing greater abundance, prosperity, and freedom. By shifting scarcity mindset and limiting beliefs around time and money, individuals open themselves up to new possibilities, financial abundance, and the freedom to live life on their own terms.

Chapter 1: Rediscovering the Power Within

In a quaint little town nestled between rolling hills and whispering forests, there lived a woman named Emily. Emily was a kind-hearted soul, always busy with the hustle and bustle of daily life. Yet, deep within her, there lingered a faint memory of a time when she believed in magic – a time when she knew that anything was possible.

One crisp autumn day, while cleaning out her attic, Emily stumbled upon an old treasure chest hidden beneath a pile of forgotten memories. With trembling hands, she brushed away the dust and opened the chest, revealing a treasure trove of forgotten relics. And there, at the bottom of the chest, lay a dusty old book – its pages yellowed with age, but its words still pulsating with life.

As Emily flipped through the pages, a wave of nostalgia washed over her. She remembered the days of her youth, when she would spend hours lost in the teachings of the mysterious book. She recalled the joy of practicing the ancient wisdom, the thrill of unlocking the secrets of the universe.

But as life got busier and the years passed by, Emily had forgotten all about the magical world within the book. She had buried it deep within her subconscious, along with her childhood dreams and aspirations. Until now.

With a sense of wonder and curiosity, Emily delved back into the pages of the book, rediscovering the timeless wisdom that had once guided her path. She learned about the power of her mind to shape her reality, the interconnectedness of all things, and the infinite possibilities that lay dormant within her.

Through the teachings of the book, Emily began to remember who she truly was – a powerful creator, capable of manifesting her deepest desires. She learned that her thoughts were like seeds planted in the fertile soil of consciousness, and that with intention and belief, she could cultivate a life filled with abundance, joy, and fulfillment.

And so, dear reader, let Emily's journey be a reminder to us all – a reminder that within each of us lies a treasure trove of untapped potential, waiting to be unearthed. Let us not forget the magic that resides within us, but instead, let us embrace it fully and create the life of our dreams.

For in the rediscovery of our inner power, we find the key to unlocking a world of endless possibilities – a world where anything is possible, if only we believe. And with that belief, dear reader, let us embark on a journey of self-discovery and transformation, as we rediscover the power within and unleash our full potential upon the world. Now get ready to take a quantum leap into the *levels of consciousness*. In the next section, we'll explore how these insights can rock our world and spark some serious transformations. So, grab your quantum cape and let's leap in!

Four Levels of Consciousness

Dr. Michael Bernard Beckwith is a renowned spiritual teacher and founder of the Agape International Spiritual Center in Los Angeles, California. His profound teachings on consciousness have inspired countless individuals around the world to awaken to their true potential and lead lives filled with purpose and meaning.

In his Life VISION Process, Dr. Beckwith outlines four distinct levels of consciousness, each representing a stage in our spiritual journey. These levels are a vibrational frequency in mind that provide a framework for understanding our relationship with the universe and offer invaluable guidance for personal growth and transformation.

As we explore Dr. Beckwith's insights on consciousness within the context of our discussion on QMS, we embark on a journey of self-discovery and enlightenment. By integrating his wisdom into our exploration of QMS, we deepen our understanding of the power of consciousness and its profound impact on our lives.

Here we will delve into each level of consciousness outlined by Dr. Beckwith, exploring how QMS can serve as a catalyst for spiritual evolution and personal empowerment. Through this synergistic approach, we open ourselves to new possibilities and unlock the limitless potential that resides within each of us by leaping levels of consciousness.

According to Dr. Michael Bernard Beckwith's Life VISION Process he outlines four levels of consciousness:

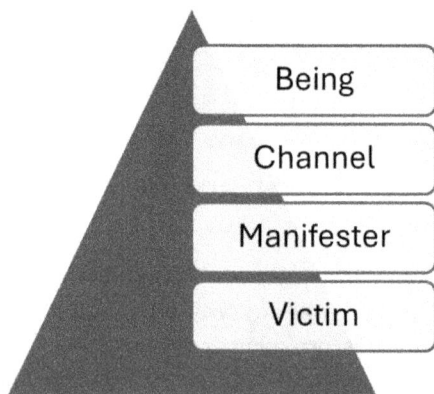

1. **Victim Consciousness**: At this level, individuals perceive themselves as victims of circumstances, believing that external factors determine their fate. They feel powerless and blame others for their challenges.

2. **Manifester Consciousness**: In this stage, individuals begin to recognize their power to shape their

reality through their thoughts, beliefs, and actions. They understand the importance of intention and take responsibility for co-creating their experiences.

3. **Channel Consciousness (Through Me):** At this level, individuals understand that they are channels for a higher power or universal intelligence to express itself. They surrender to divine guidance and allow themselves to be instruments of love, wisdom, and creativity.

4. **Being Consciousness (As Me):** This is the highest level of consciousness, where individuals experience a deep sense of oneness with the universe. They realize their inherent divinity and live from a place of love, compassion, and unity. They see themselves as co-creators with the universe and manifest their desires effortlessly.

These four levels of consciousness represent a journey of personal growth and spiritual evolution, guiding individuals towards greater self-awareness, empowerment, and alignment with their highest potential. Traversing through these 4 levels can happen naturally by default in a haphazard way or we can ascend through these levels intentionally through the use of QMS.

How do you know where you are in consciousness at any given moment?

This is a great question. The answer is simple but not easy to explain. You can be in multiple levels of consciousness throughout the day, and it is nearly impossible to be in two or more levels simultaneously in thought. Thought will travers through the levels and experiences can also travers through the levels. To provide a brief example of what it might be like to be at any specific level I have included some short stories to explain the levels in a clear way.

1. **Victimhood:** Alex wakes up feeling defeated. He missed his alarm and is now running late for work. Frustrated and overwhelmed, he blames the traffic for his tardiness. Throughout the day, Alex feels like life is constantly working against him. He perceives every setback as a personal attack, leaving him feeling powerless and resentful towards others. Alex feels that he cannot get ahead, and that the system is rigged against him. He's waiting for his lucky break. If only things in his life changed, then he would be able to be the person he wanted to be.

2. **Manifester:** Maya starts her day with a positive affirmation: "I am capable of achieving my goals." As she faces challenges at work, Maya sees them as opportunities for growth. She takes proactive steps to overcome obstacles and remains focused on her vision for success. Maya's confidence and determination lead her to take inspired action, manifesting her dreams into reality. Maya really understands that she is responsible for everything that happens in her life and is willing to take on that responsibility. She understands that by taking responsibility she doesn't give her power away to anything, anyone, or any situation. She understands that she somehow has the ability to control the results and outcomes in her life.

3. **Channel:** David practices mindfulness during his lunch break, sitting quietly in nature and observing the world around him. As he connects with the present moment, David experiences a deep sense of peace and clarity. He recognizes the interconnectedness of all things and trusts in the natural flow of life. David feels a profound sense of gratitude for the beauty and abundance that surrounds him. Davud realizes he is a channel or a puzzle piece and is being used by the forces of source itself to operate through him in his own life as well as the lives of others around him. Life is not just about him getting ahead but about everyone getting ahead.

4. **As-Me:** Emily reflects on her day with compassion and acceptance. Despite facing challenges and setbacks, she approaches each experience with grace and humility. Emily understands that life is a journey of growth and transformation, and she embraces every moment as an opportunity for learning and expansion. She feels deeply connected to the universe and recognizes her own divine nature within herself and others. Emily seems to always be lucky in her life, always in the right place at the right time. Opportunities just happen in her presence. Opportunities not just for her but also for everyone around her. The world seems to bend around her like she is magical force of nature, and she doesn't even need to say anything. She is simply a pure authentic being, pure oneness.

Leaping in Consciousness (Ascension):

Through the practice of QMS, individuals are empowered to recognize and transcend low levels of consciousness, such as victimhood or resistance, by accessing higher states of awareness. As they ascend through the levels of consciousness, they experience profound shifts (Leaps) in their perception, mindset, and behavior, leading to transformative outcomes in various aspects of their lives. We can literally leap from one level of consciousness to another. By doing this we shift our internal energetic vibration or frequency.

1. **Victimhood to Empowerment:** By shifting from a victim mentality to one of empowerment, individuals reclaim their personal power and take ownership of their lives. They no longer feel helpless or at the mercy of external circumstances but instead recognize their ability to create positive change through their thoughts, emotions, and actions.

2. **Resistance to Resilience:** As individuals release resistance and embrace resilience, they become more adaptable and

flexible in the face of challenges. They learn to flow with life's ups and downs, finding strength and inner peace amidst adversity. Rather than dwelling on setbacks, they see them as opportunities for growth and learning.

3. **Fear to Fearlessness:** By befriending & transcending fear, individuals free themselves from limiting beliefs and self-imposed barriers. They step outside of their comfort zones and pursue their dreams with courage and conviction. Fear no longer holds them back but instead becomes a catalyst for growth and exploration.

4. **Scarcity to Abundance:** Through a shift from scarcity to abundance consciousness, individuals open themselves up to a world of limitless possibilities and opportunities. They recognize the abundance that surrounds them in all aspects of life and cultivate a mindset of gratitude and abundance. As a result, they attract more abundance into their lives in the form of prosperity, joy, and fulfillment.

5. **Separation to Oneness:** As individuals transcend the illusion of separation and embrace oneness, they experience a deep sense of connection and unity with all of existence. They recognize the interconnectedness of all beings and realize that they are part of something greater than themselves. This profound shift in perception leads to greater compassion, empathy, and harmony in their relationships and interactions.

Overall, the ultimate goal of QMS is to empower individuals to recognize when they are operating from a low level of consciousness and to elevate themselves to higher states of awareness in a moment's notice. Through this practice, they unlock their full potential, experience greater fulfillment, and create a life aligned with their deepest desires and intentions.

Let's Jump into it already!

So, are you ready to embark on this journey of ascension? Get ready to dive deep into the world of QMS and unlock the true power within you!

Chapter 2: Unleashing the Quantum Power of QMS

In this chapter, we embark on a journey deep into the heart of QMS, exploring its profound implications for manifesting desired outcomes in our lives. As we delve into the mechanics of QMS, we uncover the intricate dance between consciousness, the quantum field, and the art of manifestation.

At its core, QMS is founded on the principle that our thoughts and emotions are potent forces that shape the fabric of our reality. By learning to harness the power of our minds and emotions, we can actively co-create the experiences we desire and step into our fullest potential.

Exploring the Quantum Landscape

To understand how QMS influences reality, we must first acquaint ourselves with the enigmatic realm of quantum physics. Within the quantum realm, the traditional laws of cause-and-effect dissolve into a sea of probabilities, where particles exist in a state of superposition and events unfold in a non-linear fashion. Here, everything is interconnected, and the observer plays a pivotal role in determining outcomes through the act of observation.

In the quantum field, our thoughts and emotions act as energetic frequencies that resonate with the underlying fabric of reality. Like tuning forks, they emit vibrational signals that reverberate throughout the quantum landscape, influencing the trajectory of our experiences. When we engage in QMS practices, such as affirmative prayer, visualization, and positive affirmations, we are essentially attuning ourselves to the frequencies of our desired outcomes, aligning our inner world with the external reality we wish to create.

Harnessing Power Through the Practice of Intention

Central to the practice of QMS is the cultivation of focused intention—the conscious directing of our thoughts and emotions towards a specific goal or desire. Intention acts as the guiding force that propels us towards our chosen destination, imbuing our actions with purpose and clarity.

Through the practice of intention, we can bridge the gap between our present reality and the future we envision for ourselves. By clearly defining our goals and aspirations, we set in motion a series of events that align with our intentions, drawing towards us the people, resources, and opportunities needed to manifest our dreams.

To learn more about the Powerful Practice of Intention you dive deeper into The Practice Method 30-Day Blueprint for Living Your Extraordinary Life and go to the specific practice of Intention contained within the blueprint for more detail. If you do not already have a copy of The Practice Method you can purchase it for download at a discounted rate here www.thepracticemethod.com

Embracing the Quantum Dance

As we navigate the quantum landscape, we come to recognize the intricate interplay between thoughts, emotions, and manifestation. Thoughts serve as the blueprints for our desires, providing the framework upon which our reality is built. Emotions, on the other hand, serve as the fuel that propels these blueprints into action, infusing them with the necessary energy to manifest themselves in the physical world.

When our thoughts and emotions are aligned with our desired outcomes, we create a powerful synergy that amplifies our manifesting abilities. Positive thoughts, infused with feelings of gratitude, joy, and abundance, resonate at a higher frequency, drawing towards us experiences that mirror our elevated state of being. Conversely, negative thoughts, steeped in fear, doubt, and lack, perpetuate a cycle of limitation and struggle, hindering our ability to manifest our desires.

Embodying the Quantum Shift

As we journey further into the realm of QMS, we begin to embody the principles of quantum consciousness, embracing the notion that we are co-creators of our reality. Through QMS practices, we learn to transcend the limitations of the egoic mind and tap into the infinite potential of the quantum field.

By cultivating a mindset of positivity, clarity, and abundance, we attune ourselves to the frequencies of success and fulfillment. We become conscious architects of our reality, shaping our experiences with intention and purpose. As we align with the infinite possibilities of the quantum field, we unlock the door to a life filled with joy, abundance, and limitless potential.

Stepping into Infinite Possibility

The practice of QMS offers us a profound opportunity to transform our lives from the inside out. By harnessing the power of our words, thoughts and emotions, we can transcend the limitations of the past and step into a future filled with infinite possibility.

Through focused intention, aligned with the frequencies of our desired outcomes, we can manifest our dreams with effortless ease. By embracing the principles of quantum consciousness, we can tap into the boundless creative potential of the universe and become conscious co-creators of our reality by simply speaking them into existence.

As we continue our journey into the quantum realm, let us remember that the power to shape our destiny lies within us. By embracing the principles of QMS and embodying the quantum shift, we can unlock the door to a life of joy, abundance, and fulfillment beyond our wildest dreams.

Before we can understand the step-by-steps of QMS, we need to first get authentically real with ourselves and admit what we really believe.

I can do my very best to give you the exact science of QMS, but if you do not believe that any of what I am saying is hogwash or simply downright bullshit then you will manifest that result. You really need to get this right here, and right now. The quantum is always giving you what you believe and what you think about most. The Law of Thinking states that you will get what you think most about.

The quantum doesn't care what you think about. IT is completely non-biased, non-judgmental. The IT or whatever you decide to believe it or call it doesn't care or have feelings. It doesn't know morality. In fact, IT doesn't understand the human concept of positive or negative, good or bad, moral or immoral. IT ONLY knows energy, frequency, and vibration. IT doesn't care whether or not you believe in it or not. IT doesn't judge you because you believe in it or not. Think of The Quantum as an ALL KNOWING MIND that only has one ability. This one ability is that it says YES to everything, regardless of its vibration, frequency, or energy. We (The Observers) have the ability to choose. This is the real meaning of having volition.

The Triune Nature of Reality & The Quantum Field (Quantum Creation)

The creation process of the Quantum, is life itself, is the divine itself, is the quantum itself. LIFE is ALL there is, The DIVINE is ALL there is, The QUANTUM is ALL there is.

In our exploration of the quantum realm, we encounter a concept that mirrors the Triune Nature of God, or the Creative Process as described in various spiritual teachings, including the works of Ernest Holmes. Just as in the Christian triad of Father, Son, and Holy Spirit, or Ernest Holmes and the Creative Process involving Idea, Expression, and Result, the quantum world also reveals itself in a triune manner, Quantum Creation. See Appendix A for Illustration 2.0

1. Quantum Substance: At the heart of the quantum realm lies the Quantum Substance, the foundational essence from which all manifestations arise. This Quantum Substance is akin to the divine presence or creative intelligence described in Ernest Holmes' teachings. It is the unmanifest potentiality from which all possibilities emerge. It is a Masculine energy. A Force, a Power, The Universal Consciousness. A.k.a. The God Mind

2. Quantum Foam: Surrounding and permeating the Quantum Substance is the Quantum Foam, the medium through which the Substance expresses itself. This field is like the soil in the creative process, providing the fertile ground for seeds of intention to take root and grow. It is the medium of infinite potentiality, responding to the vibrations of thought and intention. Previous sentence. It is an effervescence. A bubbling substance. That is both wave and particle. It was believed that this was what the void was. The deep infinity of nothingness. But recently Quantum scientists discovered that the nothingness is actually a whole lot of somethingness. That somethingness is quantum foam a.k.a. the fertile feminine energy. The Law of The Universal Mind. It is unbiased and non-judgmental. It can only deliver a yes in response to what is being created in the Quantum Substance.

Quantum Manifestation: Through the interaction of the Quantum Substance and Field, manifestations emerge into physical reality. This is where the intentions, thoughts, and emotions of sentient beings' interface with the quantum realm, shaping the fabric of reality. Just as the Creative Process moves from seed to soil to plant, so too does the quantum journey unfold from potentiality to manifestation. This is the demonstrated physical universe; everything we know to physically exist which emerges from the quantum substance and gets planted into the quantum foam and blossoms into a manifested reality.

Understanding this Triune Nature of Reality empowers us to recognize our role as co-creators of our experience. By aligning our thoughts, emotions, and intentions with the Quantum Substance and Field, we become active participants in the process of manifestation. Through this alignment, we harness the inherent creative power of the quantum realm to shape our lives according to our highest vision.

In the pages that follow, we will delve deeper into the practical application of this understanding through the QMS techniques, or as Ernest Holmes might refer to it, the creative process: Seed, Soil, Plant. By integrating these principles into our daily lives, we embark on a journey of self-discovery and transformation, aligning ourselves with the divine flow of creation in the Quantum Creation Model.

Words that describe the Triune Nature of Reality

In the appendix table 2.2 you will find a list of powerful description words that relate to each specific attribute within the triune nature of reality

Chapter 3: How to Use QMS: Step-by-Step (5 Steps)

In this chapter, we embark on a practical exploration of the five transformative steps of QMS. These steps serve as the blueprint for harnessing the power of our consciousness to manifest our desired outcomes and create profound shifts in our lives. Let us journey together through each step, uncovering the key principles and practices that underpin the art of QMS.

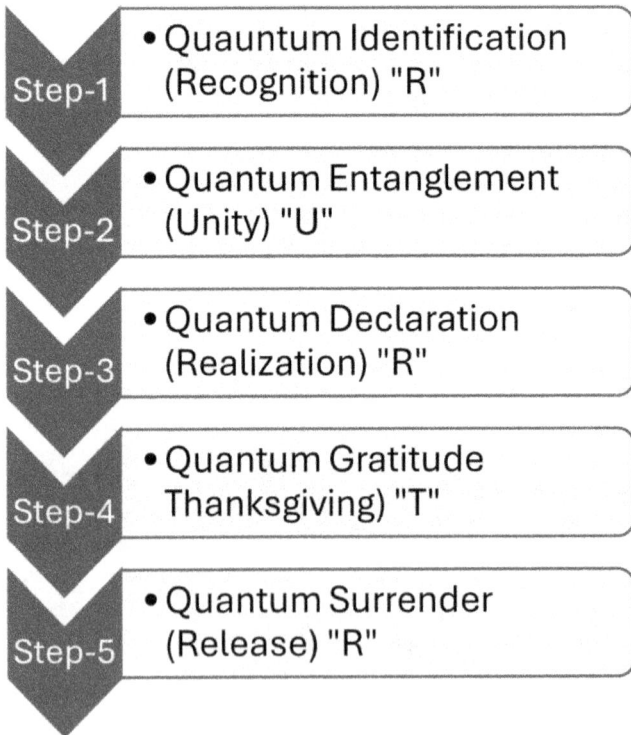

Step-1	• Quauntum Identification (Recognition) "R"
Step-2	• Quantum Entanglement (Unity) "U"
Step-3	• Quantum Declaration (Realization) "R"
Step-4	• Quantum Gratitude Thanksgiving) "T"
Step-5	• Quantum Surrender (Release) "R"

Step 1: Quantum Identification (Recognize the Quantum Source)

The journey of QMS begins with Quantum Identification, the process of identifying and acknowledging the limiting beliefs and negative thought patterns that stand in the way of our desires. Through introspection and self-awareness, we shine a light on the subconscious programming that shapes our reality, bringing it into the conscious mind for examination. By recognizing the thoughts and beliefs that no longer serve us, we pave the way for transformation and growth.

In Step 1 of QMS, we explore the essence of the divine quantum substance, a force that imbues the universe with Harmony, Love, Abundance, Freedom, and countless other positive descriptors. This substance is often conceptualized as Divine Order, Divine Action, or Divine Orchestration, embodying qualities of omniscience, omnipresence, and all-powerfulness. It serves as the perfect commander-in-chief, directing the intricate dance of life with precision and wisdom. Like a skilled conductor guiding an orchestra to create harmonious music, the divine quantum substance orchestrates the symphony of the cosmos, ensuring that every note is played in perfect alignment with the grand design of creation. As we deepen our understanding of this divine essence, we come to recognize its omnipotent presence in every aspect of our lives, guiding us toward our highest good and ultimate fulfillment. In this step we recognize the all-ness of the qualities and the omni presence of these qualities of the quantum source. Clearly recognizing these qualities is a very important step and cannot be skipped in the process of QMS.

The recognition step of QMS is simply to declare the absolute truth about the divine source of the quantum itself. I have created an appendix-A Table 1.1 to help you find words to help you will recognition of the Source Quantum or Almighty Deity to help you construct your own QMS. Below you will find an example with some short phrases or words that work sufficiently.

Example: *"I know and recognize that there is a power and presence of abundance, wholeness, it is everywhere, IT is OMNIPRESENT, IT is OMNISCIENCE, IT is PERFECT, IT is HARMONIOUS, IT is SYCHRONIZED, IT is LOVE & CREATION itself. IT is ALL of LIFE"*

Below, you'll find a section where you can jot down all the characteristics you perceive to be divine from your source. Take your time to reflect on the qualities that resonate with you and describe them in your own words. This exercise is designed to help you deepen your understanding and connection to the divine quantum substance as you progress through your QMS journey. If you have a specific faith, then you can direct all the qualities that you believe exist from your faith in your divine source.

_____
_____
_____
_____
_____
_____
_____
_____
_____
_____
_____
_____
_____
_____
_____
_____
_____
_____

Step 2: Quantum Entanglement (Unify Yourself with The Quantum)

In the second step of QMS, Quantum Entanglement, we establish a deep connection with our desired outcomes, aligning our thoughts, emotions, and intentions with the frequencies of success and abundance. Through the practice of visualization and affirmative prayer, we immerse ourselves in the experience of our desired reality, cultivating a sense of excitement, gratitude, and anticipation. By entangling our consciousness with the quantum field, we set the stage for manifestation and creation.

In Step Two, we delve into the concept of Quantum Entanglement, which essentially implies that you are intricately connected to the divine quantum substance. Imagine yourself as a thread woven into the fabric of the universe – you are not separate from it, but rather entangled with it in a beautiful dance of existence. This entanglement means that every thought, feeling, and action you emit resonates throughout the quantum field, influencing the tapestry of reality in profound ways. Recognizing this interconnectedness allows you to embrace the truth that you are an integral part of the cosmic symphony, and your participation in it is both inevitable and essential. Through QMS, you'll learn to harness the power of this entanglement to manifest your deepest desires and align with the divine flow of creation.

As you explore the concept of Quantum Entanglement, you realize that you are not just an observer of the universe; you are an active participant in its grand design. Embrace phrases like "You are one with the ONE" and "You ARE; That you are" as reminders of your inherent connection to the divine quantum substance. Understand that if this substance is everywhere present, then you must be one with it, and it must be one with you. This realization fills you with a sense of awe and wonder, knowing that your thoughts, emotions, and actions reverberate throughout the cosmos, influencing the unfolding of reality. You are entangled with the fabric of existence, woven into the tapestry of life in a harmonious dance of interconnectedness. This understanding empowers you to navigate the quantum field with confidence and intention, knowing that your presence and participation are vital components of the cosmic symphony.

In your own words, affirm your entanglement with the divine quantum substance by declaring statements such as "I am one with the ONE," "I AM; That I am," and "If it is everywhere present, then I must be one with it, and it must be one with me." Let these affirmations resonate within you, reinforcing your connection to the vast and intricate web of existence.

Example: *"Since the Quantum is EVERYWHERE present, then that means IT must BE where I AM, I AM ONE with the ONE Quantum Field, I AM entangled with it, and all of its attributes are ONE with me. There is no separation from IT, My LIFE is IT, IT is my LIFE NOW"*

Take a moment to reflect on the profound realization of your entanglement with the divine quantum substance. Recognize the significance of this connection and how it shapes your perception of reality and your place within it. As you prepare to capture your thoughts on paper, allow yourself to bask in the awareness of your inherent oneness with the universe. Then, in the space provided below, express your personal insights, feelings, and affirmations regarding your entanglement with the divine quantum substance. Let your journaling serve as a sacred practice of reaffirming your connection to the cosmic fabric of existence.

_____
_____
_____
_____
_____
_____
_____

Step 3:
Quantum Declaration (Realization)

Next, we move into the step of Quantum Realization/Declaration, where we declare our intentions to the universe with unwavering conviction and certainty. Through the power of spoken word and affirmative declaration, we affirm our desires as already fulfilled, speaking them into existence with clarity and authority. By embodying the energy of our desired outcomes and speaking them into reality, we initiate the process of manifestation and manifestation.

In this crucial step, we embrace the power of Quantum Realization/Declaration. Here, we boldly declare our intentions to the universe with unwavering conviction and certainty. Through the transformative force of spoken word and affirmative declaration, we assert our desires as already fulfilled, speaking them into existence with clarity and authority. By embodying the energy of our desired outcomes and vocalizing them as present realities, we initiate the profound process of manifestation and creation.

Through Quantum Realization/Declaration, we harness the inherent power of our words to shape our reality, aligning ourselves with the frequencies of abundance, success, and fulfillment. With each declaration, we strengthen our connection to the quantum field, amplifying the signals of our intentions and propelling them towards manifestation. As we speak our desires into existence, we cultivate a deep sense of empowerment and alignment, knowing that our words have the power to shape the course of our lives.

This step serves as a pivotal moment in our journey of QMS, marking the transition from mere intention to tangible manifestation. By embracing the practice of Quantum Realization/Declaration, we step into our role as conscious creators, actively shaping our reality with each word we speak. With unwavering belief and conviction, we affirm our inherent power to manifest our deepest desires, inviting abundance, joy, and fulfillment into every aspect of our lives.

In this step we are describing the plant or the body of reality. For example, if you were to describe a rose to the universe as something you wanted to create, how would you describe it. You would describe its beauty, its intoxicating aroma, its delicateness, its thorns of protection, its fabulous shades and variety of colors, its hardiness and ability to thrive in the right environment. This is what the 3rd-step of QMS is all about. You are going to describe in full detail what you want by answering the question "What would you Love?"

There is a special way to describe what you would love. Answer the question in the present tense, as though it has already happened, use 1st person language for yourself. Have it be meaningful, and emotionally positive. This is your VISION of Life for the desired result, goal, or dream you are looking to achieve in your life with the help of the infinite (which you are, already)

If you need help with this step, I have two resources available for you.

The PRACTICE METHOD: There is an entire section of The PRACTICE Method- 30-Day Blueprint for Living Your Extraordinary Life that is devoted to the practice of REALIZATION on Page-57 (Day-6). If you do not have the book, you can download it in PDF format by going to www.thepracticemethod.com

FREE REALIZATION MEDITATION: I also have an entire Episode on Podcast devoted to REALIZATION Meditation practice.

https://tinyurl.com/Realization-Meditation

If you are curious if you can use QMS to do sessions for others, then answer is yes, and that is not the intention of this book. If you want more information on how to use QMS for others as a QMS professional, you can reach out to me via email at theo@theotilton.com

For purposes of keeping this light and easy for the moment simply use the space below to describe in detail the future state of what you want your life/situation/desire dream to be like. Use all of your sense right now to think about what you would LOVE. And then use the space provided to write it down.

For example:

"I am fully energized and excited every morning to start my day. I am moving my body and doing all the actions needed to achieve my goals and dreams. Every day is exciting and I see myself at my perfect ideal weight and waist size. I am confident and I am getting noticed. All of my friends and family are noticing all the changes I have made and I and giving my body what it needs through movement and exercise. My bodyfat is on the way to my perfect ideal body composition of 11% Bodyfat. I am stronger than I have ever been in my entire life and I maintain this amazing health with ease and grace. As if by a miracle my body has healed everything that wasn't in alignment with my true nature of me being whole, healthy, and complete. My body temple's muscles, bones, organs, blood, tissues and composition are now all working together synergistically for my highest and greatest version of myself, the way God (The universe, Jesus, Buddha) intended. I am a divine specimen of what it is to be a perfectly whole human, and I love myself and take care of myself deeply on every level."

Use the following section to write out your realization of truth:

_____
_____
_____
_____
_____
_____
_____
_____
_____
_____
_____
_____
_____
_____
_____
_____
_____
_____
_____
_____
_____
_____
_____
_____
_____
_____
_____
_____
_____
_____
_____

Step 4:
Quantum Gratitude (Thanksgiving)

In the fourth step of QMS, Quantum Thanksgiving and Gratitude, we express heartfelt gratitude for the blessings and abundance that already exist in our lives, as well as for the manifestations that are on their way. Through the practice of gratitude, we align ourselves with the vibrational frequencies of abundance and appreciation, attracting more blessings into our lives. By acknowledging the abundance that surrounds us and expressing gratitude for it, we open the floodgates for even greater blessings to flow into our lives.

Example: in this moment right here, right now, I am filled with gratitude and appreciation for all of the miracles. The awe and wonder that fills me now, knowing that the Quantum realm is now aligning and conspiring to demonstrate my greatest good has me humbled and grateful. Thank you, God (Jesus, Universe).

Use this section to practice writing out gratitude: Use words like gratitude, grateful, thank you, appreciation, heart filled with happiness and joy. It is about feeling and emotion. Imagine your realization was truly manifested. What would it feel like?

_____

_____

_____

_____

_____

_____

_____

_____

_____

_____

_____

Step 5: Release and Surrender

Finally, we come to the fifth and final step of QMS: Release and Surrender. In this step, we surrender our desires to the wisdom of the universe, trusting that our intentions have been heard and that the process of manifestation is underway. By letting go of attachment and releasing any resistance or doubt, we create space for miracles to unfold in our lives. Through the practice of surrender, we allow the universe to orchestrate the details of our manifestations, knowing that everything is unfolding in divine timing and perfect order.

This is probably the simplest step, however, not necessarily easy to actually do. Why? you might be wondering. Well, it is easy to say thank you, like the previous step, but now you are going to release and surrender your words over to the authority of the quantum(God, Jesus, Buddha, etc.) the Living Law that ONLY knows how to say YES to you and your request. The Quantum Foam or the Medium, a.k.a. the LAW is non-biased, non-judgmental, it has no opinion, it doesn't have morality, it simply says YES all of the time to you it also doesn't understand negation NOT's. So why is this hard to do. Well, it's not that it is hard to do but more that we might not want to truly let it go. I mean, really let it go.

It's a matter of SURRENDERING & TRUSTING the Quantum (God, etc.) to take your request and begin to deliver it. This is the BIGGEST Kept secret behind the secret. We all understand that the Law of Attraction is about Ask, Believe, Receive. And that we attract what we are, not what we want. And there is another piece that many do not dive deep into and that is Surrender and Know it is really done. This is where you begin to act as if.

For example, when I started writing my international best-selling book, The PRACTICE Method. I used the Power of QMS to see the future I wanted. I AM in International Best-Selling Author, and I write best-selling books and I impact 1000's of people's lives. I would say, I now release and surrender this new truth over to the universe and I allow it to be. I give it to the Living Law that only says YES to me, and I surrender over to God all the mechanics of how it will be done. And So, It Is! AMEN!

12-months later I was an International Best-Selling Author. Along the way, I found a book coach, I learned different writing styles. An idea for a book popped into my head almost as if by divine download I wrote the book in 4-months and I was nervous but I never wavered from my belief that what I put out there was going to happen.

It is in the release and surrender that the quantum foam does what it does. If we keep looking and saying it's not happening fast enough, or it doesn't look the way we think it should look. What we are really doing is interrupting the quantum with doubt, worry, fear, and new updated ideas. Basically we keep conflicting with our dream. This is a sure-fire way to not demonstrate what you want. So when I say, that the surrender step is very basic but. so the most important step. I mean tit! Please take this seriously, otherwise you will F@$& it up!

Your release can be super easy, and simple like this. don't make it complicated. "I release, I let go, I surrender my words over to the Law of the quantum knowing it is already done. And So, It Is! Amen."

It's your turn. Write out a release statement.

_____
_____
_____
_____
_____
_____
_____
_____
_____
_____

Helpful TIP:

Easy way to remember the 5 steps…

Acronym for the steps **R.U.R.T.R.**

Steps:

Recognition

Unity

Realization

Thanksgiving

Release

Word Association:
 R=ARE, U=YOU, R=READY, T=TO, R=RECEIVE

Chapter 4: Overcoming Life's Challenges with QMS Scripts

Welcome to Overcoming Life's Challenges with QMS, a powerful tool to guide you through life's toughest situations with unwavering belief and deep emotional resonance. Within these pages, you'll discover written-out examples of QMS scripts meticulously crafted to evoke profound feelings of belief and empowerment.

Purpose:

The purpose of this section is to empower you to overcome life's obstacles with absolute conviction and heartfelt emotion. Each QMS script is infused with affirmations, declarations, and visualizations designed to resonate deeply within your soul, igniting a flame of unwavering belief in your ability to transform your reality.

How to Use This Section:

1. **Identify Your Challenge:** Take a moment to connect with the challenge you're facing. Whether it's financial struggles, relationship turmoil, or health concerns, acknowledge it fully and without judgment.

2. **Select the Relevant QMS Script:** Browse through the chapter and select the QMS script that speaks directly to your challenge. As you read through the script, allow yourself to feel the words wash over you, stirring up emotions of confidence, hope, and determination. Feel free to substitute anything related to the identification of the Quantum with your personal belief in a higher power. If you want to use the word God, or Jesus, of any other divine beingness; go right ahead. QMS is not a tool to dissuade you from your current belief, rather a tool to enhance the effectiveness of your current

prayer practices.

3. **Read and Internalize:** Dive into the chosen script with your whole being. Feel the power of each affirmation resonating deep within your core, as if they were already manifesting in your reality. Embrace the emotions that arise as you visualize your desired outcome with vivid clarity.

4. **Practice Regularly:** Make a commitment to practice the selected QMS script daily, immersing yourself in its transformative energy. As you recite the prayers, embody the emotions of belief, gratitude, and joy, knowing that your desires are already on their way to you. Ernest Holmes says in Science of Mind "Treat Until You Demonstrate"

5. **Monitor Your Progress:** Keep a journal to track your progress and observe any shifts in your thoughts, feelings, and circumstances. Notice how your beliefs begin to align with your desires and celebrate every small victory along the way. You will notice changes and transformations occurring. It might seem as though nothing is happening until it does and then you will experience the bliss of knowing the real reason why your life's experience transformed as if by a miracle.

With unwavering belief and heartfelt emotion, you hold the power to rewrite your story and manifest your greatest dreams. As you engage with the QMS scripts in this chapter, allow yourself to fully embrace the transformative journey that lies ahead.

Health & Wellbeing:

1. Anxiety
2. Chronic Pain
3. Depression
4. Digestive Issues
5. Fatigue
6. Insomnia
7. Migraines
8. Stress

Love & Relationships:

1. Breakup
2. Communication Issues
3. Divorce
4. Infidelity
5. Loneliness
6. Relationship Strain
7. Self-Love
8. Trust Issues

Career & Vocation:

1. Burnout
2. Financial Strain
3. Lack of Purpose
4. Procrastination
5. Unfulfilling Job
6. Work-Life Balance

Freedom of Time & Money:

1. Debt
2. Lack of Abundance
3. Limited Time
4. Overwhelm

Health & Well-Being

1. ## Anxiety:

    I embrace the truth that I am infinitely connected to the boundless harmony and peace of the quantum realm. In this present moment, I effortlessly align with the divine order and tranquility that permeates my being. I declare with unwavering conviction that anxiety has no power over me, as I am anchored in the serene essence of my true self. With profound gratitude, I affirm the release of any remnants of anxious energy to the expansive universe. I surrender fully to the natural flow of harmony and ease, knowing that my reality is one of calm and serenity. And so, it is   .

2. ## Chronic Pain:

    I embody the truth of perfect health and vitality that flows abundantly from the quantum field. In this eternal now, I align effortlessly with the divine healing energy that courses through every cell of my being. I declare with absolute certainty that pain is but a fleeting illusion in the face of my inherent wholeness. With deep gratitude, I release any lingering discomfort to the vast expanse of the universe. I surrender completely to the innate intelligence of my body, trusting in its inherent ability to restore balance and well-being. And so, it is.

3. ## Depression:

    I embrace the infinite love and joy that emanate from the quantum source, knowing that I am eternally connected to the boundless light within. In this sacred moment, I align effortlessly with the radiant brilliance of my true nature, transcending all shadows of sadness and despair. I declare with unwavering conviction that depression holds no power over me, as I am anchored in the profound joy of my soul. With heartfelt gratitude, I release any lingering shadows to the vastness of the universe. I surrender fully to the abundant joy and peace that flows through me, knowing that my reality is one of unbridled happiness. And so, it is.

4. Digestive Issues:

I embody the truth of perfect balance and harmony that permeate the quantum realm, knowing that I am infinitely connected to the divine intelligence of my body. In this present moment, I align effortlessly with the optimal functioning of my digestive system, transcending all discordant energies and imbalances. I declare with absolute certainty that my body is a temple of vibrant health and vitality. With profound gratitude, I let go of any persistent thoughts of disharmony to the expansive universe. I surrender completely to the natural rhythm of my body, trusting in its innate ability to maintain equilibrium and nourishment. And so, it is.

5. Fatigue:

I embrace the boundless energy and vitality that flow endlessly from the quantum field, knowing that I am eternally connected to the wellspring of life itself. In this eternal now, I align effortlessly with the divine vitality and stamina that course through every fiber of my being. I declare with unwavering conviction that fatigue is but a temporary illusion in the face of my inherent vibrancy. With deep gratitude, I let go of any ruminations of tiredness or lethargy to the vast expanse of the universe. I surrender fully to the natural flow of energy and rejuvenation, knowing that my reality is one of boundless vitality. And so, it is.

6. Insomnia:

I embody the truth of deep and restorative sleep that emanates from the quantum realm, knowing that I am infinitely connected to the divine peace and tranquility within. In this eternal now, I align effortlessly with the profound serenity and relaxation that envelops my being. I declare with absolute certainty that insomnia has no power over me, as I am anchored in the tranquil depths of my soul. With profound gratitude, I discharge any frequency or feeling of restlessness or sleeplessness to the vast expanse of the universe. I surrender completely to the natural rhythm of sleep and restoration, trusting in its innate ability to nurture and revitalize me. And so, it is.

7. **Migraines:**

I embrace the truth of perfect health and harmony that permeate the quantum field, knowing that I am eternally connected to the divine healing energy within. In this present moment, I align effortlessly with the optimal functioning of my mind and body, transcending all discordant energies and imbalances. I declare with unwavering conviction that migraines are but a temporary illusion in the face of my inherent well-being. With deep gratitude, I release any remnants of discomfort or pain to the expansive universe. I surrender fully to the natural balance and harmony of my being, trusting in its innate ability to restore equilibrium and vitality. And so, it is.

8. **Stress:**

I embody the truth of perfect peace and serenity that flow endlessly from the quantum realm, knowing that I am infinitely connected to the boundless tranquility within. In this eternal now, I align effortlessly with the divine calmness and relaxation that envelop my being. I declare with absolute certainty that stress has no power over me, as I am anchored in the tranquil depths of my soul. With profound gratitude, I release any remnants of tension or anxiety to the vast expanse of the universe. I surrender completely to the natural flow

Love & Relationships:

1. **Breakup:**

I embrace the eternal truth of love and connection that

permeates the quantum fabric of the universe. In this sacred moment, I align effortlessly with the boundless love that flows through every aspect of my being. I declare with absolute certainty that the dissolution of a relationship is but a temporary transition in the journey of my soul. With profound gratitude, I release any indication of sorrow or heartache to the expansive universe. I open up completely to the healing power of love, knowing that my heart is available for new beginnings and infinite possibilities. And so, it is.

2. Communication Issues:

I embody the divine essence of clear and harmonious communication that emanates from the quantum source. In this eternal now, I align effortlessly with the sacred flow of authentic expression and understanding. I declare with unwavering conviction that communication barriers dissolve in the presence of my open heart and receptive mind. With deep gratitude, I release any tethers of misunderstanding or discord to the vast expanse of the universe. I submit fully to the transformative power of open and honest communication, knowing that my relationships thrive in the space of mutual respect and empathy. And so, it is.

3. Divorce:

I embrace the eternal truth of divine love and unity that transcends all human experiences and circumstances. In this sacred moment, I align effortlessly with the infinite wisdom and compassion of the quantum field. I declare with absolute certainty that the end of a marriage is but a chapter in the ever-unfolding story of my soul's evolution. With profound gratitude, I release any remnants of pain or resentment to the boundless universe. I surrender completely to the healing power of love, knowing that I am supported and guided on my journey toward wholeness and fulfillment. And so, it is.

4. Infidelity:

I embody the divine essence of trust and fidelity that emanate from the quantum realm of infinite possibilities. In this eternal now, I align effortlessly with the sacred bond of love and commitment that unites souls in harmony and respect. I declare with unwavering conviction that betrayal is but a temporary illusion in the face of the eternal truth of love. With deep gratitude, I dissolve any thorns of hurt or betrayal to the expansive universe. I avail myself fully to the transformative power of forgiveness and compassion, knowing that my heart is open to healing and renewal. And so, it is.

5. Loneliness:

I embrace the eternal truth of interconnectedness and belonging that pervades the quantum tapestry of existence. In this sacred moment, I align effortlessly with the infinite love and companionship that surround me at all times. I declare with absolute certainty that loneliness is but a passing shadow in the radiance of my inner light. With profound gratitude, I release any remnants of isolation or longing to the boundless universe. I surrender completely to the divine flow of love and connection, knowing that I am never alone on my journey through life. And so, it is.

6. Relationship Strain:

I embody the divine essence of harmony and understanding that emanate from the quantum field of infinite possibilities. In this eternal now, I align effortlessly with the sacred dance of give and take that nurtures healthy relationships. I declare with unwavering conviction that strains in relationships are but opportunities for growth and deeper connection. With deep gratitude, I release any remnants of discord or tension to the expansive universe. I surrender fully to the transformative power of love and compassion, knowing that my relationships flourish in the soil of mutual respect and empathy. And so, it is.

7. Self-Love:

I embrace the eternal truth of my inherent worthiness and

divine essence that reside within the depths of my being. In this sacred moment, I align effortlessly with the boundless love and acceptance that flow from the quantum realm. I declare with absolute certainty that I am worthy of love, compassion, and self-care in all aspects of my life. With profound gratitude, I release any remnants of self-doubt or criticism to the expansive universe. I surrender completely to the nurturing embrace of self-love, knowing that I am whole and complete just as I am. And so, it is.

8. Trust Issues:

I embody the divine essence of trust and faith that emanate from the quantum field of infinite possibilities. In this eternal now, I align effortlessly with the sacred knowing that all is well and unfolding for my highest good. I declare with unwavering conviction that trust issues are but temporary barriers to the deeper connection and intimacy that await me. With deep gratitude, I release any remnants of fear or doubt to the expansive universe. I surrender fully to the transformative power of trust and vulnerability, knowing that I am supported and guided on my journey toward deeper connections and authentic relationships. And so, it is.

Career & Vocation:

1. Burnout:

In this sacred moment, I embrace the eternal truth of balance and vitality that flows through the quantum field of infinite possibilities. I align effortlessly with the boundless energy and passion that fuel my soul's purpose and mission. I declare with absolute certainty that burnout is but a temporary state in my journey toward fulfillment and abundance. With profound gratitude, I release any remnants of exhaustion or overwhelm to the expansive universe. I surrender completely to the rejuvenating power of self-care and alignment with my true passions, knowing that I am supported and guided on my path to vitality and joy. And so, it is.

2. **Financial Strain:**

I embody the divine essence of abundance and prosperity that permeate the quantum fabric of the universe. In this eternal now, I align effortlessly with the infinite flow of wealth and resources available to me. I declare with unwavering conviction that financial strain is but a temporary illusion in the face of the eternal truth of abundance. With deep gratitude, I release any remnants of scarcity or lack to the expansive universe. I surrender fully to the abundant flow of money and opportunities, knowing that I am a magnet for prosperity and success. And so, it is.

3. **Lack of Purpose:**

I embrace the eternal truth of purpose and fulfillment that reside within the depths of my being. In this sacred moment, I align effortlessly with the divine guidance and wisdom that illuminate my path. I declare with absolute certainty that my life is imbued with meaning and purpose, and every experience serves to enrich my soul's journey. With profound gratitude, I release any remnants of doubt or confusion to the boundless universe. I surrender completely to the clarity and direction that flow from my connection to the quantum field, knowing that I am guided toward my highest expression of self. And so, it is.

4. **Procrastination:**

I embody the divine essence of focus and productivity that emanate from the quantum realm of infinite possibilities. In this eternal now, I align effortlessly with the creative flow that propels me toward my goals and aspirations. I declare with unwavering conviction that procrastination is but a temporary obstacle on my path to success and fulfillment. With deep gratitude, I release any remnants of resistance or hesitation to the expansive universe. I surrender fully to the momentum of inspiration and action, knowing that I am empowered to accomplish all that I desire. And so, it is.

5. **Unfulfilling Job**:

I embrace the eternal truth of alignment and fulfillment that permeate the quantum tapestry of existence. In this sacred moment, I align effortlessly with the perfect opportunities for growth and expansion in my career. I declare with absolute certainty that my ideal job is already on its way to me, filled with purpose, passion, and fulfillment. With profound gratitude, I release any remnants of dissatisfaction or frustration to the boundless universe. I surrender completely to the unfolding of divine timing and synchronicity, knowing that I am guided toward the work that nourishes my soul and uplifts my spirit. And so, it is.

6. **Work-Life Balance**:

I embody the divine essence of harmony and equilibrium that emanate from the quantum field of infinite possibilities. In this eternal now, I align effortlessly with the perfect balance between my professional endeavors and personal well-being. I declare with unwavering conviction that work-life balance is my natural state of being, where joy and fulfillment abound in every aspect of my life. With deep gratitude, I release any remnants of stress or overwhelm to the expansive universe. I surrender fully to the rhythm of life, knowing that I am supported and nurtured in all that I do. And so, it is.

Freedom of Time & Money:

1. ## Debt:
   In this sacred moment, I align with the eternal truth of abundance and prosperity that permeate the quantum field of infinite possibilities. I declare with unwavering certainty that debt is but a temporary illusion in the face of the boundless wealth available to me. With profound gratitude, I release any remnants of financial burden or scarcity to the expansive universe. I surrender completely to the flow of abundance and prosperity, knowing that I am supported and guided on my path to financial freedom. And so, it is.

2. ## Lack of Abundance:
   I embody the divine essence of abundance and prosperity that flow abundantly through the quantum fabric of the universe. In this eternal now, I align effortlessly with the infinite wealth and resources available to me. I declare with absolute conviction that lack is but a temporary illusion in the face of the eternal truth of abundance. With deep gratitude, I release any remnants of scarcity or limitation to the expansive universe. I surrender fully to the flow of abundance and prosperity, knowing that I am a magnet for wealth and success. And so, it is.

3. ## Limited Time:
   I embrace the eternal truth of time as a fluid and expansive dimension that exists beyond the constraints of the clock. In this sacred moment, I align effortlessly with the boundless flow of time and opportunity available to me. I declare with unwavering certainty that time constraints are but a temporary illusion in the face of the

infinite possibilities that await me. With profound gratitude, I release any remnants of limitation or pressure to the expansive universe. I surrender completely to the flow of time and opportunity, knowing that I am guided toward my highest expression of self. And so, it is.

4. **Overwhelm**:

I embody the divine essence of peace and clarity that emanate from the quantum realm of infinite possibilities. In this eternal now, I align effortlessly with the perfect balance and harmony that dissolve overwhelm and stress. I declare with absolute conviction that overwhelm is but a temporary state in the face of the eternal truth of inner peace. With deep gratitude, I release any remnants of chaos or confusion to the boundless universe. I surrender fully to the flow of tranquility and ease, knowing that I am supported and nurtured in every moment. And so, it is.

I am going to be working on a larger array of life challenges and coming up with QMS Treatments for all of them. If you would like access to this valuable resource as it becomes available go to the bonus material website link here:

www.quantummindshifting.com/bonuses

Chapter 5: B.Y.O.Q. Build Your Own QMS

This chapter is your gateway to quantum empowerment and manifesting independence for the rest of your life, where you'll immerse yourself in the exhilarating process of crafting your own QMS leaps. Here, you'll embark on a journey of self-discovery and transformation as you harness the infinite power of your words and thoughts to manifest your deepest desires and intentions. With unwavering belief and gratitude, you'll explore the boundless possibilities of the quantum field, aligning your reality with your wildest dreams. Get ready to step into your true potential and manifest with absolute certainty and conviction, as you unlock the secrets of the universe within

1. Identify what you want to resolve, heal, fix, transform, get more of...

_____
_____
_____
_____
_____
_____
_____
_____
_____
_____
_____
_____
_____
_____
_____
_____

2. What do you want it to be like? (What will it look like, feel like, sound like, use your senses) use positive present tense language as though it has already happened – (You'll be using this in the Quantum Realization step)

_____
_____
_____
_____
_____
_____
_____
_____
_____
_____
_____
_____
_____
_____
_____
_____
_____
_____
_____
_____
_____
_____
_____
_____
_____
_____
_____

3. What's the CORE ATTRIBUTE or HIGHER TRUTH of the Challenge? (Abundance is Everywhere Present, Love is ALL there IS, Harmony Permeates ALL, everything is Whole & Complete As it Is, Order, Speed/Velocity, Freedom, Wellness)

_____
_____
_____
_____
_____
_____
_____
_____
_____
_____
_____
_____
_____
_____
_____
_____
_____
_____
_____
_____
_____
_____
_____
_____
_____

Now that you know the CORE ATTRIBUTE & The Way you want the RESULT to be we can start building your very own QMS Scientific Prayer.

Step-1 Recognize the Quantum:

What do you recognize and declare as quantum qualities (Qualities of the Source that you will pull into your experience)?

Example: God is All there is, God is ONE with the ONE, The Quantum is LOVE, JOY, PEACE, and Harmony. The Universe is held together with the omni presence of this Love.

_____
_____
_____
_____
_____
_____
_____
_____
_____
_____
_____
_____
_____
_____
_____
_____
_____
_____
_____
_____
_____
_____
_____
_____
_____
_____
_____
_____

Step-2 Quantum Entanglement:

Describe how you are entangled and connected and unified to the source quantum power/God?

Example: IF this power and presence is everywhere, then it must be where I AM. I AM ONE with this LOVE, I AM ONE with the ONE, All of its power is entangled with the being that I AM right now in this moment.

_____
_____
_____
_____
_____
_____
_____
_____
_____
_____
_____
_____
_____
_____
_____
_____
_____
_____
_____
_____
_____
_____
_____
_____
_____

Step-3 Quantum Realization:

Use from bullet#2 (**What do you want it to be like? (What will it look like, feel like, sound like, use your senses)** use positive present tense language as though it has already happened. *After you have written this down. Go perform the Mirror Time-Machine Exercise in Appendix-B*

_____

_____

_____

_____

_____

_____

_____

_____

_____

_____

_____

_____

_____

_____

_____

_____

_____

_____

_____

_____

_____

_____

_____

_____

_____

Step-4: Quantum Gratitude:

Share with feelings and words of gratitude as though the future manifestation has already happened, right now. How grateful are you?

_____
_____
_____
_____
_____
_____
_____
_____
_____
_____
_____
_____
_____
_____
_____
_____
_____
_____
_____
_____
_____
_____
_____
_____
_____

Step-5 Quantum Release

In your own words, let go of your words as a request over to the quantum universe.

_____
_____
_____
_____
_____
_____
_____
_____
_____
_____
_____
_____
_____
_____
_____
_____
_____
_____
_____
_____
_____
_____
_____
_____
_____
_____
_____

For a PRINTABLE Empty QMS prayer form that you can use to repeat this process until you are fully versed and memorize all the steps will be made available in the bonus section.

Go to **www.quantummindshifting.com/bonuses**

Put it all together in one cohesive QMS prayer paragraph below.

After completing each of the individual steps, it's time to synthesize your QMS leap into one powerful and cohesive session. Combining the elements of quantum identification, unity, declaration, gratitude, and release into a single narrative, you'll create a potent affirmative QMS prayer that resonates with the truth of your being and the infinite potential of the quantum universe. This unified declaration will serve as your personal mantra, empowering you to embody your desired reality with unwavering conviction and alignment.

Get ready to witness the transformational power of your words as you quantum leap into the life of your dreams!

_____
_____
_____
_____
_____
_____
_____
_____
_____
_____
_____
_____
_____
_____
_____
_____
_____
_____

The Experiment:

Clients from all over the world use QMS and don't even know they are doing it. You might argue with me but hear me out. Just like Ernest Holmes stated in "Science of Mind" we are 'walking prayers', basically what he means by this is we are always praying. Whether we like it or not or believe it or not, we are always thinking and speaking and emoting, and believing something and this level of consciousness is always creating our life 24/7. Thank goodness there is a time delay in the creation process of what it is to be human.

To use this process consciously is what I am asking you to do for at least 30-days. Commit yourself to using QMS for the next 30-days. Do QMS at least 1x per day for one specific area of your life and do it consistently and repeatedly. What you repeatedly do forges a pattern in your subconscious mind. And your subconscious mind is your personal Law. Leaping in consciousness as a permanent way of being may not be possible however if we practice regularly, we will at least have a chance of realigning our consciousness at least once per day. And the more we do this. The more we stay in alignment with the parallel future of our future selves we want to manifest. Do this for 30-days and I want to hear back from you. Connect with us and let us know how your experiment is going and what miracles have happened. Share with the Collective on Facebook

🔗 https://www.facebook.com/groups/qmscollective/

Bonus Steps:

Contained within this book there are the how-to steps for the 5-steps of QMS Leap Scripts and these steps are effective an 80% of the time. And, if you happen to be struggling with doubt, worry, fear, disbelief, resistance, limiting beliefs, there's a 7-step protocol that is modeled after Ernest Holmes Spiritual Mind Treatment technology to be able to handle any doubt, denial, dis-belief, etc. If you are interested in learning about the 7-step process, I am building an online QMS Course that will be available in the future; you can jump into the online course materials coming soon available here at :**www.quantummindshifting.com**

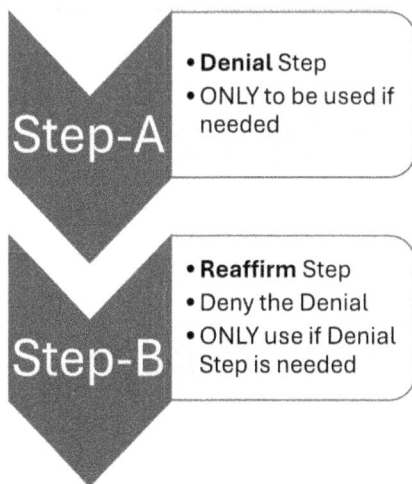

Step-A
- **Denial** Step
- ONLY to be used if needed

Step-B
- **Reaffirm** Step
- Deny the Denial
- ONLY use if Denial Step is needed

It's Your Turn to Practice

As we draw the curtains on this profound exploration into the boundless realm of QMS, let's take a moment to reflect on the transformative journey we've embarked upon together. Throughout this book, we've delved into the depths of quantum physics, ancient wisdom, and cutting-edge scientific prayer methods, uncovering the secrets to unlocking our true potential and manifesting our deepest desires.

From the very beginning, we set out on a quest to understand the fundamental principles of QMS: quantum identification, unity, declaration, gratitude, and release. These foundational steps have served as our guiding light, illuminating the path to manifestation mastery and empowering us to create the lives we've always dreamed of.

But beyond the theoretical framework lies the heart of QMS— the belief that we are co-creators of our reality, and that our thoughts and words have the power to shape the world around us. Through the stories, exercises, and intentional spiritual fiction shared in this book, we've witnessed firsthand the transformative power of aligning our consciousness with our deepest intentions and desires.

Imagine, for a moment, standing at the edge of a vast ocean, with the shimmering horizon stretching out before you. Each wave represents a thought, a word, a belief, rippling out into the infinite expanse of the universe. With each deliberate intention and heartfelt prayer, you send out a ripple of energy, setting in motion a chain of events that reverberates throughout the cosmos.

In this ocean of infinite possibilities, you are the captain of your ship, navigating the currents of consciousness with clarity, purpose, and intention. As you chart your course through the turbulent waters of life, remember that you possess the power to steer your vessel in any direction you choose.

But manifestation mastery isn't just about setting sail—it's about weathering the storms that inevitably arise along the way. Like a seasoned sailor, you must learn to navigate the choppy waters of doubt, fear, and uncertainty, anchoring yourself in the unshakable belief that you are divinely guided and supported every step of the way.

And so, as we bid farewell to this journey of exploration and discovery, let us carry forth the wisdom and insights gleaned from these pages into our daily lives. Let us practice QMS with unwavering faith and conviction, knowing that with each deliberate thought and intentional word, we are co-creating a reality that is in perfect alignment with our deepest desires.

As you close the book and step back into the tapestry of your everyday existence, remember that the power to manifest lies within you. Embrace the teachings of QMS, embody its principles with every fiber of your being, and watch as your wildest dreams unfold before your eyes.

And should you ever find yourself adrift in the sea of life, uncertain of your next move, remember this: you are never alone. Reach out to the QMS Collective, a community of like-minded souls committed to supporting one another on the journey of manifestation mastery. And stay tuned for the upcoming online course at www.quantummindshifting.com, where you'll receive personalized guidance and support as you continue your journey of transformation.

With boundless gratitude and infinite possibility, I invite you to take the leap into the extraordinary life that awaits you. The universe is conspiring in your favor, dear reader—dive deep, dream big, and let your light shine bright.

Are you ready to embrace the magic of QMS and manifest your most extraordinary life?

Your adventure begins now!

Appendix-A:

Table 1.1

Qualities of The Quantum Substance

Words that can be used to describe and articulate within your QMS to describe the source in Step-1

Omnipresence, Omniscience, Omnipotence, All-knowing, Everywhere-present, Divine Order, Divine Action, Divine Operation, The Matrix, Timeless Source, Everything/Nothing, Father/Mother/God, Holy Source, Universal Energy, Limitless Field of Possibilities, Spirit, Power, Life, Action, Wholeness, Truth, Love, Beauty, Intelligence, Law, First Cause, Thought, Seed, Creator, Force of Life, Divine Energy Wave, Universal Wisdom, Universal/Divine Consciousness

Table 2.2

Quantum Substance
Spirit, Power, Life, Action, Wholeness, Truth, Love, Beauty, Intelligence, Law, First Cause, Thought, Seed, Masculine, Force, Wave, Wisdom, Consciousness, Objective
Quantum Foam
Soul, Medium, Receptivity, Will, Imagination, Subjectivity, Pattern, Memory, Consciousness, Belief, Reflection, Soil, Feminine, Law, Receiver, Effervescence, Yes, Subjective, Mind Subconscious,
Quantum Manifestation
Body, Result, Objectification, Manifestation, Concrete form, Matter, Effect, Expression, Sensation, Form, Experience, Plant, Demonstration, Particle, Physical, Reality, Universe, Atom, Conditions, Circumstances, Situations, Effect, Human

Appendix-B:

Quantum Time Machine - Mirror Exercise - Crafting Your Vision and Identifying Limiting Beliefs

Preparation for the Time Machine:

- **Time Travel:** You are about to go 3 years into the future using your bathroom mirror. This will be an exercise in imagination, creativity, playfulness, and diving into the power of the quantum realm through expression of our words as though they are really real!

- **Clarity is Power:** Before you start, you will want a very clear VISION/MISSION/REALIZATION written down from Step-3. If you do not have a clear VISION/REALIZATION yet. You will need to do this first by answering the question "What Would You Love? In Step-3" Realization. Be clear and precise details of your VISION pf Life and use all of your senses. Write it down in first person. I AM. Think about it in another way. Imagine everything you have ever wanted/desired has happened. All of it: The House, Car, Life, Spouse, Love, Finances, Job, Career, Freedom, Vacations, Healing, Health, Well-Being.

- **Memorize**: If you have your Realization/VISION ready. Read it to get clear on the details for yourself. Once you have read it to yourself and you understand the basic elements of what you want to say. You are basically ready for the Quantum Time-Machine.

Exercise: Quantum Time Machine

- **Be in front of a Mirror:** Pretend your reflection is your current self and you're about to embark on a 3 year trip into the future. Stare into your reflection's eyes. Say to your reflection Have a Good Trip!

- **Turn around counterclockwise:** In 3 steps turn around counter clockwise. Once you stop counter spin in 3 steps you will be back at your reflection. Pretend that you are now 3-years in the future. And you are seeing your old self from 3-years earlier.

- **Pretend that Future you is meeting past you:** greet your reflection with excitement as soon as you see your reflection. "OMG it is so nice to see you! It's been so damn long, 3-years, can you believe it?"

- **Pretend your old self in the reflection asks you a question:** Reflection asks: "It's been 3-years, wow, what has happened in your life? What are you doing and being nowadays?"

- **Answer with enthusiasm for about 1-3 minutes:** Start with "Well, have I got a story for you. I am so happy and grateful. You won't believe what has happened!" Then continue to answer with everything in your life that has happened. Share from the snapshot perspective. *Do not share how it happened. Rather just that you are living this life right now.* State in the present tense. What does it look like, smell like, taste like, sound like, be descriptive. *Remember this reality has happened and you are sharing it with your past self.*

- **Your Life Looks Good on You:** Once you are completed stating your realization/new reality. Whisper to yourself as though your reflection is whispering... say "That's amazing! Your life looks so good on you" Reply back with "Thank you, it was great seeing you"

- **Memorize the Feeling and Energy:** After the thank you. close your eyes and memorize the feeling of your body sensations, energy, feel the excitement and joy. Hold this feeling as long as you can. And when you open your eyes. Stare deep into the eyes of your reflection and say, "And So It Is!"

Self Evaluation

- **Assess Belief and Limitations:** Once you have written down your vision/realization, review each aspect and self-evaluate. Do you believe this is possible? If not, why?

- **Identify Limiting Beliefs:** Identify any doubts, fears, or limiting beliefs that arise as you review your vision or perform the Time Machine. You might experience thoughts like: "I'm not good enough," "I don't deserve success," or "It's too hard to achieve."

- **Apply QMS:** For each identified limiting belief, use QMS techniques & practices to help shift your consciousness and align your beliefs with your desired reality. This may involve doing other self-love tools like affirmations, visualization, gratitude practices, or forgiveness exercises. For more information on many of these additional practices. Get The PRACTICE Method: 30-Day Blueprint for Living Your Extraordinary Life" and work through your shit with a heart of compassion and self-love. www.thepracticemethod.com

- **Revisit and Revise:** I Encourage you to revisit your vision/dream/realization regularly, refining and adjusting it as needed. Continuously assess and address any new limiting beliefs that arise along the way. And practice QMS daily.

Glossary:

Here's a glossary of terms associated with QMS, quantum physics, and related concepts within this book:

1. **Quantum Mind Shifting (QMS):** A spiritual and transformative practice that combines principles of quantum physics with affirmative prayer to shift consciousness and manifest desired outcomes.

2. **Quantum Physics:** The branch of physics that deals with the behavior of matter and energy at the smallest scales, such as atoms and subatomic particles, where the principles of quantum mechanics apply.

3. **Quantum Mechanics:** The scientific theory that describes the behavior of matter and energy on the atomic and subatomic scale, characterized by phenomena such as wave-particle duality, superposition, and entanglement.

4. **Superposition:** A quantum mechanical principle stating that a particle can exist in multiple states simultaneously until it is measured or observed, at which point it collapses into a single state.

5. **Entanglement:** A phenomenon in quantum mechanics where two or more particles become correlated in such a way that the state of one particle instantaneously affects the state of the other(s), regardless of the distance between them.

6. **Observer Effect:** The concept in quantum physics that the act of observing or measuring a particle affects its

behavior, potentially altering its state or properties.

7. **Wave-Particle Duality:** The principle in quantum mechanics is that particles, such as electrons and photons, exhibit both wave-like and particle-like properties depending on how they are observed or measured.

8. **Manifestation/Demonstration:** The process of bringing desired outcomes or experiences into reality through intention, belief, and visualization, often associated with spiritual or metaphysical practices.

9. **Affirmative Prayer:** A form of prayer or meditation that focuses on affirming positive outcomes, often used in spiritual and religious contexts to manifest desired results.

10. **Consciousness:** The state of awareness or subjective experience often considered fundamental to the understanding of reality and the manifestation of intentions.

11. **Vibration:** The frequency at which energy oscillates, believed to play a role in the manifestation of reality and the attraction of desired outcomes.

12. **Alignment:** The state of harmonizing one's thoughts, beliefs, and actions with one's desires and intentions, facilitating the manifestation process.

13. **Intention:** A focused and deliberate desire or goal, often used in manifestation practices to clarify desired outcomes and direct energy towards their realization.

14. **Gratitude:** A feeling of thankfulness or appreciation, often utilized in manifestation practices to amplify positive emotions and attract abundance.

15. **Synchronicity:** The occurrence of meaningful coincidences or events that appear to be interconnected, often interpreted as signs of alignment with one's desires or spiritual guidance.

16. **Oneness:** The philosophical or spiritual concept that all things are interconnected and part of a unified whole, often associated with mystical experiences and enlightenment.

About the Author

As a Mindset Coach, Theo Tilton can help you design and manifest a life that's in harmony with your Soul's purpose. Theo inspires and empowers all those that are drawn to him to live their highest vision in the context of love and joy. His passion is teaching clients to unlock their true potential, achieve outrageous success, and live a life they LOVE living! Theo is an International Best-Selling author, inspiring speaker, passionate educator, certified life coach, and a highly sought-after transformational mindset & Mind Shift coach.

For over 15 years, Theo has worked with spiritually-minded, heart-centered individuals, entrepreneurs and health & wellness enthusiasts, helping them build their dreams, accelerate their results, and create richer, more fulfilling lives. He had a 25-year career in software development and product ideation as well as a 20+ year side career as an international fitness instructor and personal trainer.

He's shared the stage with Mary M Morrissey, and Matt Boggs. He also the creator of The Blueprint of Living an Extraordinary Life Podcast available wherever you listen to your favorite shows and has been seen on multiple episodes of the TV Talk Show "Family Today with Maria Mircovich."

Theo believes that we are all connected in this thing we call Life and that it is completely possible to transform any area of life through your mindset. "Change your thinking, transform your life."

Additional Links

Want a digital Version of this book:

Get it here link>>> www.quantummindshifting.com

Paperback available on Amazon

Bonus Material:

www.quantummindshifting.com/Bonuses/

Other Titles from Author:

The
PRACTICE Method™

30-Day Blueprint for Living Your Extraordinary Life

Get it here: www.thepracticemethod.com

TPM Online 30-Day Program

Join the ONLINE coaching Program for The PRACTICE Method

www.thepracticemethod.com

Connect with the author on social media

- **Official Website**: www.theotilton.com
- **Email Theo** at theo@theotilton.com
- **Meta Business Page**:
  www.facebook.com/TheoTiltonCoaching
- **Instagram** @TheoTilton
  https://www.instagram.com/TheoTilton/
- **LinkedIn** @TheoTiltonCoaching
  https://www.linkedin.com/in/TheoTiltonCoaching

References:

1. HOLMES, E. (1926). THE SCIENCE OF MIND. NEW YORK: DODD, MEAD & CO.
2. TILLER, W. (2007). SCIENCE AND HUMAN TRANSFORMATION: SUBTLE ENERGIES, INTENTIONALITY AND CONSCIOUSNESS. WALNUT CREEK, CA: PAVIOR PUBLISHING.
3. BECKWITH, M. B. (2006). LIFE VISIONING: A FOUR-STAGE EVOLUTIONARY JOURNEY TO LIVE AS DIVINE LOVE. SOUNDS TRUE.
4. DAVISSON, C. J., & GERMER, L. H. (1927). REFLECTION OF ELECTRONS BY A CRYSTAL OF NICKEL. PHYSICAL REVIEW, 30(6), 705–740.
5. DE BROGLIE, L. (1924). RECHERCHES SUR LA THÉORIE DES QUANTA (RESEARCH ON THE THEORY OF QUANTA). ANNALES DE PHYSIQUE, 10(3), 22–128.
6. EINSTEIN, A., PODOLSKY, B., & ROSEN, N. (1935). CAN QUANTUM-MECHANICAL DESCRIPTION OF PHYSICAL REALITY BE CONSIDERED COMPLETE? PHYSICAL REVIEW, 47(10), 777–780.
7. GRANGIER, P., ROGER, G., & ASPECT, A. (1986). EXPERIMENTAL EVIDENCE FOR A PHOTON ANTICORRELATION EFFECT ON A BEAM SPLITTER: A NEW LIGHT ON SINGLE-PHOTON INTERFERENCES. EUROPHYSICS LETTERS, 1(4), 173–179.
8. HEISENBERG, W. (1927). ÜBER DEN ANSCHAULICHEN INHALT DER QUANTENTHEORETISCHEN KINEMATIK UND MECHANIK (ON THE PERCEPTUAL CONTENT OF QUANTUM THEORETICAL KINEMATICS AND MECHANICS). ZEITSCHRIFT FÜR PHYSIK, 43(3–4), 172–198.
9. SCHRÖDINGER, E. (1935). DISCUSSION OF PROBABILITY RELATIONS BETWEEN SEPARATED SYSTEMS.

Proceedings of the Cambridge Philosophical Society, 31, 555–563.

10. Stern, O., & Gerlach, W. (1922). Der Experimentelle Nachweis der Richtungsquantelung im Magnetfeld (The Experimental Proof of Space Quantization in a Magnetic Field). Zeitschrift für Physik, 8(1), 110–111.

11. Aspect, A., Dalibard, J., & Roger, G. (1982). Experimental Test of Bell's Inequalities Using Time-Varying Analyzers. Physical Review Letters, 49(25), 1804–1807.

12. Wheeler, J. A., & Zurek, W. H. (1983). Quantum Theory and Measurement. Princeton University Press.

13. Young, T. (1804). The Bakerian Lecture: Experiments and Calculations Relative to Physical Optics. Philosophical Transactions of the Royal Society of London, 94, 1–16.